Binary Options:

Making Money With

A Complete Quick Start Guide for Beginners: Strategies and Best Practice to Trade Successfully

© Copyright 2016 - All rights reserved.

In no way is it legal to reproduce, duplicate, or transmit any part of this document in either electronic means or in printed format. Recording of this publication is strictly prohibited and any storage of this document is not allowed unless with written permission from the publisher. All rights reserved.

The information provided herein is stated to be truthful and consistent, in that any liability, in terms of inattention or otherwise, by any usage or abuse of any policies, processes, or directions contained within is the solitary and utter responsibility of the recipient reader. Under no circumstances will any legal responsibility or blame be held against the publisher for any reparation, damages, or monetary loss due to the information herein, either directly or indirectly.

Respective authors own all copyrights not held by the publisher.

Legal Notice:

This book is copyright protected. This is only for personal use. You cannot amend, distribute, sell, use, quote or paraphrase any part or the content within this book without the consent of the author or copyright owner. Legal action will be pursued if this is breached.

Disclaimer Notice:

Please note the information contained within this document is for educational and entertainment purposes only. Every attempt has been made to provide accurate, up to date and reliable complete information. No warranties of any kind are expressed or implied. Readers acknowledge that the author is not engaging in the rendering of legal, financial, medical or professional advice.

By reading this document, the reader agrees that under no circumstances are we responsible for any losses, direct or indirect, which are incurred as a result of the use of information contained within this document, including, but not limited to, — errors, omissions, or inaccuracies.

Table of Contents

Introduction 1

Chapter 1: The Fundamentals 4

Chapter 2: Financial Juggling 18

Chapter 3: Tailoring Binary Options 31

Chapter 4: Tools and Strategies 41

Chapter 5: Getting Started 50

Chapter 6: Tips, Tricks, and Temperament 60

Conclusion 72

Introduction

I want to thank you and congratulate you for downloading the book *Binary Options Trading: Making Money With.* On the surface, binary options trading appears to be one of the easiest active financial investments for newcomers to break into it. While it certainly is less complicated than day trading and options trading, binary options require knowledge, strategy, and instinct. That is where *Binary Options Trading* comes in.

This book contains proven steps and strategies on how to become a truly successful binary options trader. While reading, you will learn the basics of options trading, how to balance risk and reward, as well as learn about various strategies and the attitude necessary to become profitable in the long-term. In addition, this book details tips for getting started in the business and how to do more than just keep your head afloat.

Here's an indisputable fact: you will need to give yourself a deep and broad education regarding binary options trading in order to become successful. Often times neophyte traders quit within a few years because they did not understand the true implications of trading, which are that you need dedication, time, flexible strategies, and extreme resilience to make it in this market. When it comes to trading, success and failure depend solely upon the individual and even the best binary options traders have bad days. Whether you can learn from those bad days and adapt is what will make you a good trader. However, this will not happen overnight.

If you do not develop your knowledge of binary options, it is possible that luck will carry you to success for a short while. However, that will inevitably end, and so prospect traders must develop their knowledge and skills to the best of their abilities. This book can provide the beginnings of a solid binary options education that will help you to determine whether you have what it takes to become a professional trader. Those who have experienced long-term success in this field have gained the financial freedom to do many things, such as quit their day job, pay off the mortgage early, and expand their portfolio in order to branch out into other modes of trading. With the right skills and mindset, you can accomplish this too.

It's time for you to become an amazing binary options trader. Read on to discover the basics, secrets, and tips to trading that will set you on the path to success and financial autonomy.

Chapter 1: The Fundamentals

Like all other trades, success begins with an understanding of the basics. While binary options are relatively simple to grasp, an investor's prosperity is based on his or her understanding of the rules and ability to strategize within those confines. Thus, this chapter aims to lay out the essentials of binary options trading and a few of the investment opportunities available to traders.

What are Binary Options?

Binary options is a financial agreement represented by a particular security in which the investor believes that the security will close either above or below a certain strike price at the time of the options' expiration.

Investors are in-the-money when they purchase a call option, and it closes above the strike price or when they sell a put option, and it closes below the strike price. An investor is out-of-the-money when he purchases a call option, and it closes below the strike price or when he sells a put option, and it closes above the strike price. The price at which a security is purchased or sold depends on the bid/ask price.[1]

For anyone, who is not accustomed with the financial language, this may sound rather confusing. Here are a few clarifying definitions.

- **Security**: This represents whatever the investor is trading, such as a particular company's stock or an index like the Dow Jones.

- **Call**: This is an option that is purchased.

- **Put**: This is an option that is sold.

- **Strike Price**: This is the current price of the security when the option is bought or sold. For example, if company XYZ's stock is currently worth $115 when a trader decides to purchase a call option on that security, then $115 is the strike price.

- **In-the-money**: This is when the investor has gained a profit.

- **Out-of-the-money**: This represents when an investor has lost.

- **Bid/Ask Price**: This can be a little tricky to navigate. The bid price is how much an investor can sell the stock for and the ask price is how much a buyer will pay. This fluctuates on a scale that will be discussed in further detail in the next chapter.

- **Expiration date**: This is determined depending upon the time frames that the individual trader deals in. Expiration dates can be within an hour, day, or week of a security being purchased.

Perhaps the most important point of binary options is that gain and loss is limited. Unlike day trading or options trading where loss potential is often unlimited and gains can reach incredible highs, binary options is limited based on the potential $100 profit. This means that every binary option will close with either a $100 or $0 profit/loss. However, this may be multiplied depending upon if the investor is dealing with multiple binary options under the same security at the same time. While this may seem to make binary options a relatively safe avenue of active investment, the losses can add up very quickly if investors are not cautious.

This is where the simplicity of binary options lies: the investor only needs to determine whether a security will rise or fall above or below its current value. In order to determine this, investors should be paying attention to the financial news, notably publications such as the *Wall Street Journal* and any reliable online sources. Additionally, it is paramount that investors make a study of time charts, examining where the all time highs and lows of a security lie as well as the averages. Sometimes it will be obvious when a security is about to plummet, such as when it is currently extremely high and the probability of it rising are doubtful at best. With enough practice, investors should be able to make qualified predictions regarding the market and thus limit their losses and increase profits. However, investors are advised to not listen to everything they hear; often gossip can influence the market because traders are relying upon false information to make moves. Savvy investors do their best to avoid this and only act on reliable news.

How Do Binary Options Work?

Because binary options only require the investor to speculate whether the value of a security will move up or down, the calculations for determining profit or loss is fairly simple. Here are a few examples of what can happen when trading binary options (fees are not calculated).

1. Suppose an investor is considering a stock for company XYZ that is currently worth $1,000, which is the strike price. The investor believes the price is about to plummet and so he decides to sell an option for the bid price of $32. If the stock closes beneath the original strike price, the investor will gain the $32. However, if the price climbs above the strike price, the investor will have lost $68 since the stock closed at the $100 profit ($100-$32=$68).

2. Here is a reverse example. The investor trusts that the price of the stock from company XYZ will rise and so buys the stock for the ask price of $73. If the investor is right and the stock closes at the expiration date above $1,000 for $100, then the investor will have a $27 profit since the other $73 is canceled out by the price to purchase the stock. Had the investor purchased the stock and then the priced dropped, his loss would be capped at the $73 used to buy the stock.

In order to actually trade binary options, investors will need to determine multiple elements of the trade, which are as follows.

- **Security**

    It is wise for investors to only trade with securities they are already familiar with. For example, someone who was not familiar with commodities would be foolish to try and place a call option for oil. If that same person is well versed in technology, than he or she should be working within that realm. Of course, it is possible to branch out into other areas, but only after extensive and careful research.

- **Call or Put**

    This is where the studying of charts comes in handy. By becoming familiar with the movements of the market, traders can make an educated guess as to whether the market will move up or down and therefore can determine whether to enter into a call or put option agreement. A good overall rule to follow is that if the trader is unsure of where the market will move, he or she should not place the call/put. That is a sure fire way to lose money and practicing such methods in the long-term can lead to extremely precarious financial situations. Successful binary options traders achieve financial lucrativeness by always being informed, trusting their instinct, and making calculated decisions.

- **Expiration Time**

The trader can determine his or her own time frame depending on preference. Traders can deal with something as short as a five-minute time frame to a three-month time frame. However, because binary options are such a win/loss scenario, it is often better to deal with longer time frames, with an hour being the shortest. Predicting the movement of a security within an hour can be difficult enough; attempting to predict movements that occur within a matter of minutes can be equated to gambling and should only be taken on by experienced traders.

- **Exit Strategy**

Every trader should have this in place, no matter how confident or experienced he or she is. The beauty of exiting within binary options trading is that a trader may exit at any time and does not have to wait until the expiration of the security. For example, if a trader has decided to buy a call option and the security rises above the strike price, they are in-the-money. If they predict, however, that the security price will fall below the strike price before the expiration date, they can exit the option early, collecting the profit and escaping the loss.[2] It should be noted thought that this strategy must oftentimes be set up beforehand with a broker and may not be an available option when dealing with over-the-counter options.

Once the first three elements have been determined, the trader can enter either a call or put option. Depending upon the brokerage or platform the trader is using, he or she may have an exit plan in place that will allow for an early exit.

Types of Binary Options

The types of binary options available for trading are split into four groups: stocks, indices, commodities, and currency/forex trading.[3] All of these include different types of securities that will require individual research and, in some cases, different skill sets.

- **Stocks**

    This will probably be the most familiar to novice traders. Investors can trade on any number of stock exchanges, such as The New York Stock Exchange, The London Stock Exchange, and The Tokyo Stock

Exchange. Once a stock exchange has been selected, traders may choose to purchase stock from a company that trades on that exchange.

- **Indices**

These are really a subpart of the stock market, but are listed here regardless because they are so prevalent in trading. Popular indices include the S&P 500, the Dow Jones Industrial Average, and NASDAQ. For example, stock for the technology company Apple is traded on the NASDAQ Global Select Market. However, unlike trading with a stock exchange in which someone is physically making the trader's calls and puts once called in, indices such as NASDAQ is done completely electronically.

- **Commodities**

Commodities fall into four categories: energy, metals, livestock, and agriculture.[4] Different trading platforms may offer only some or all of these

15

categories to trade on. Like other options, commodities are traded by predicting whether the price will rise or fall above or below the strike price. However, trends can be difficult to predict if the trader is not already familiar with a particular commodity.

- **Currency/Forex**

Forex stands for the foreign exchange market. Thus, someone who trades on these platforms is dealing with the fluctuating value of currency and those who are adept at predicting market movements may even be able to trade different currencies against each other.

While these are all popular means of trading binary options, it should be clear which ones are suitable to neophyte traders. It is worth noting that traders will need to be careful not to lose track of time zones and thus, their securities. This can easily be taken care if one is aware and always paying attention to the market. Although it may seem confusing at first, constant review of these facts, observation of the market, and practice trading can make a dedicated novice into an expert trader.

Chapter 2: Financial Juggling

Since the profits of binary options are capped at $100, the only way to increase profit revenue is to take part in multiple binary options contracts at once. This is incredibly appealing to those who seek to make fast fortunes through trading, but should be approached with caution. Handling multiple contracts at one time can quickly confuse inexperienced traders and cost them the money they had hoped to earn plus more. At a more elementary level, making money trading binary options requires the handling of several trades at once and, once the trader has become more experienced, may require handling several trades that are overseen by various exchanges. Entering and exiting multiple contracts can quickly become confusing and end in dramatic loss for those who lack proficiency in binary options trading. Thus, it is crucial to learn financial juggling.

How to Earn Money

A key element for success when starting out in binary options trading is for traders to not get ahead of themselves. For many, it is just too easy to get caught up in the excitement of a winning trade and the prospect of earning abundant sums of money, but becoming swept up is in fact the right way to crush dreams of trading success. Instead, traders will need to enter the playing field with a complete knowledge of what they are getting into and with a clear strategy in mind.

There are multiple elements that make up a winning strategy, including, but not limited to, preparation and proper bookkeeping. Each master plan will vary depending upon the trader. What makes a predetermined approach so valuable is that the investor is not entering into a contract blindly. Here are some components and explanations for an efficacious strategy.

- **Preparation**

Readers are already beginning to accomplish this first point by reading this book. However, preparation cannot end here. Those who wish to become successful binary options traders will need to read as much reputable literature as it is possible to get one's hands on. Once an investor has gained a thorough knowledge of binary options, it is necessary to remain up-to-date on all important and relevant financial news and laws. Lastly, traders should make a study of the time frame charts regarding the security they are interested in.

- **Know the Market**

    As stated earlier, a successful trader knows the market he or she is dealing with. Traders should work within fields that they are already familiar with since they will be able to predict trends more easily than someone who is unfamiliar with the security. While some may say that anyone can learn to read the charts, neophyte investors should consider this scenario: a former airline pilot decides that he wants to begin trading stocks. While he is not an athlete and does not know anything about sports, he has always found Nike intriguing and so decides to begin trading binary options for Nike's stock. Unfortunately, although he has studied month's worth of time frame charts, the pilot is unaware that an emerging competitor has been driving Nike's stock to an all time low for the past year and soon causes the popular company to go bankrupt. The pilot has now lost out on any options contract that he purchased prior to the bankruptcy and has probably bet incorrectly on any completed transactions. The moral of the story: even a new trader has particular knowledge about a specific field and the pilot probably should have invested in airlines for a starter.

- **Enter and Exit**

Traders should know which entrances and exits they want to take before actually making a trade. Since trades work on time frames, it would be wise to plan all contracts ahead of time consequently to not become caught up in the excitement of a last minute upsurge in a trend only to lose money when it reverses. Having an entrance planned out allows the trader to keep a cool head and having an exit planned can keep losses relatively low.

- **Bookkeeping**

    As the day goes on, traders should keep a trading diary. This will help traders to 1) keep track of wins and losses, and therefore their capital, 2) keep track of trades occurring simultaneously and 3) visualize where they are going wrong. The last point is especially important because if a trader is paying close enough attention to his or her losses, then he or she will be able to correct mistakes and keep from losing money in the future.

Risks

While it has been stated before, the rule to not go into binary options trading unprepared warrants reiterating. For anyone, who is not so familiar with the world of investment, trading can be rightly associated with gambling. To begin trading without studying and practicing first would be equivalent to doing so. The good news here is that proper preparation is possible with the right resources. These resources, such as technical indicators and simulators, will be further discussed in later chapters.

However, putting aside questions of preparedness, it can be generally agreed upon that binary option is a rather simple mode of trading. This is because it only requires that the trader decide if a trend will rise or fall in regards to the current strike price and losses are limited. Regardless of the accessibility of binary options trading, while limited losses of say $40 each may not be imposing on an individual's capital, it can add up to be a significant amount in the long run.

Even using the safest methods, trading is fraught with opportunities for failure. Happily, monetary risks are limited, since binary options always results in either a $0 or $100 profit and the most a trader can lose is

$100 minus the gained price of the stock. Risk becomes increased when traders decide to purchase or sell a group of options. For example, suppose that a trader purchases five binary options contracts for $300 at $60 a piece at a strike price of $1,500. Assume that the trader has not set up an exit strategy with his or her brokerage ahead of time and that the price of the option begins to fall after it's initial rise. Then, at the expiration time, the option closes at a strike price below $1,500. This means that the trader gains $0 and instead has lost the $300 he or she paid to acquire the options.

The good news is that that is as bad as it can get, even when taking selling puts into account. Examine this trade again, but this time take the perspective of the investor who sold the options. Had the investor sold them for a grand total of $300 and the market price rose above the strike price instead of below it (because the investor would not have sold the options if he or she did not believe the market price would fall), the investor would have a net loss of $200. This is due to the $0 or $100 profit/loss, wherein the buyer of the options is in-the-money $500 since the market moved in his favor for all 5 contracts. Therefore the seller, who sold the options for $300, has lost out on $200.

Thus, it becomes clear that bundle packages of options is just a means of dealing with larger sums of money and so require extreme confidence on the part of the trader that the market will move in the predicted direction. For beginners, it is recommended to only deal with individual contracts until sufficiently experienced.

Risk versus Reward

Investment is a game of numbers and thus it makes sense to determine the probabilities of risk and reward and then compare them. Again, due to the relative simplicity of binary options trading, there is an easy way to begin assessing probability, and that is by being aware of the 0-100 scale.

Imagine a 0-100 scale with a marker in the middle at 50. When the majority of traders believe the market is going to move in a particular direction, they will usually make similar moves, either purchasing or selling securities which will in turn influence the market moves. This then influences the bid/ask price. When the traders believe the market is going to rise, the bid/ask prices will be on the upper end of 50. In reverse, when the majority of traders believe the market price will fall below the current strike price, the bid/ask price is on the lower end up 50. It only hovers around 50 when traders are not sure which way it will move.

This is an extremely helpful tool when predicting how a market will move. However, readers should be warned that this is not a fool proof tool. While it is true that the market is influenced by the actions of its investors, people also tend to work with a herd mindset. Often, when a severe market move is made or the market suddenly becomes volatile, investors worry that they have missed some indicator and begin to do what they see everyone else doing, whether that be selling or buying puts and calls. This brings up an important component of a successful traders attitude: an investor must trust his or her instincts. While this may sometimes end badly for the investor, it is better for the investor to have been wrong on his or her own account than miss out on an opportunity because he or she was too afraid of losing to follow their gut.

The other factors of risk vs. reward are completely up to the individual investor's discretion. Before trading at all, a potential investor must determine if he or she has the capital to trade. This means the money an investor is willing to put aside just for trading and must include payment for fees due to brokerages. The capital should have enough monetary value that even if a new trader loses 10 trades in a row, it will not break the bank. Of course, if a trader loses out on 10 options in a row, than he or she should either do a serious strategy evaluation or rethink binary options trading altogether. One of the worst positions a trader can find themselves in is to run through his or her entire capital and find themselves broke. Preparing financially will be a huge asset when entering the world of trading and provide new investors with the necessary time to learn and improve.

One of the other major deciding factors regarding success in trading is whether or not the investor has the patience, time, and dedication to succeed. Binary day trading usually takes place over short time frames and thus requires attention in order to be properly managed. If new investors do not have the time for this, then it may be wise to investigate hiring a broker that can do the majority of the workload on behalf of the trader. While time may be managed, patience and dedication are requirements since no fortune was made over night.

Chapter 3: Tailoring Binary Options

When binary options come to mind, most people think of numbers. It's completely logical to do so, but an investor knows that trading is not as clean cut as that. This is one motive why people succeed at binary options trading, and others do not, and the reason goes further than the elements of a prosperous trader that have been already been stated. To become successful at trading binary options, it is not enough to just follow the rules; investors must be able to personalize them.

Tailoring Options

This book has already gone over the types of binary options available for trading, which include stocks, indices, commodities, and currency/forex. However, since the goal here is to come up with viable options for beginners, it would be best to discard the last two options. That leaves investment newcomers with stocks and indices, which, depending upon the perspective, are more or less the same thing. This is because indices can be made up of lists of the most popular stocks on the market versus a stock exchange may contain any number and variety of stocks regardless of their volatility, popularity, or accessibility. The terminology of trading on stock exchanges versus indices will come into play when selecting what is best for the individual.

So what is best? That will depend upon the existing trading abilities of the beginner and his or her interests. If the individual does have some background in trading, such as taking an active part in the growth of a mutual fund, then he or she may want to look into trading on a stock exchange using different stocks that may be a bit less well known and will help to diversity his or her profile. However, if the individual has no experience in investment, which is more likely to be the case, then it may be better to either trade on indices with extremely well-known stocks or to select well-known stocks from a stock exchange. In addition to this, there is a third option: depending upon the brokerage or platform the individual is trading on, it is possible to get a package deal that will allow the individual to trade on both the stock exchange and indices at the same time.

When selecting a platform, take into consideration which stocks to use. Again, investors should start out only trading on stocks with which they are familiar. Readers should determine their familiarity with companies by examining their lives: what products is the reader familiar with, whether that is technology, transportation, sports, energy, or healthcare? Additionally, take time zones into account. If a trader is living in Seattle but is trading on The New York Stock Exchange, then he or she will either need to be at the computer and ready to call the broker at 6:30am Pacific time or set up an automatic trader to begin the process when the bell rings on the exchange floor in New York. Although this latter option can be helpful, it is always best for a trader to look at the data personally.

Another factor that may play into selecting options is to examine time frame charts. This can be somewhat difficult because oftentimes companies will only allow someone to study the charts after the individual has become a customer. The positive note is that most reputable brokerages have access to a wide variety of stocks to choose from and so new investors should hopefully be able to select suitable stocks without examining the charts. However, once a trader has access to them, he or she should study them in order to determine which stocks have the highest rate of volatility. Stocks that make larger moves may prove easier to predict or at least have a higher chance of producing a result within a short span of time. However, traders should be warned that while this can be a practical method, it is also an ambitious one since trends can reverse themselves, especially in volatile climates. Consequently, establishing an exit point beforehand is recommended.

Above all, options should be limited to companies that interest the individual. If an investor is getting into binary options trading in order to make money and not because they love it then trading can be extremely difficult. Things will be easier if the investor chooses companies that are appealing. If a new investor loves the finance world then well-suited stocks will only make the process of reaping rewards more enjoyable.

Opportunities to Win

This is just one of the more difficult aspects of being a binary options trader. Usually, binary options only involve a yes or no choice: yes the trend will rise above the strike price or no, it won't. Spotting binary options trading opportunities, however, takes constant active participation on the trader's part. In order to take advantage of the opportunities the market provides; one must keep their ear to the financial ground.

An ideal way to do this is with newspapers. Investors should read financial sections of newspapers every day whether online or in print. Over time investors develop a preference for particular periodicals, but a wide range will help to broaden new investors' knowledge and make them more able to spot potential market indicators. Some may question the practicality behind reading the entirety of the financial news when only a portion of it may be directly related to the investor's interests, but the truth is that the financial world is deeply interconnected. If a trader is dealing in healthcare stocks, a huge fluctuation in another area such as homeownership could have a drastic effect on the stocks. It is always better to be aware of the whole financial picture and then hone in on a specific point than only be knowledgeable of one area. Additionally, it is just as important to see how a market closes for the day, as it is to see how it opens.

An effective investor should be aware of financial news all day, not just in the morning.

An additional way to stay in touch with the financial world is through websites and blogs. Some great ones include Google Finance and CNN Money. A great financial resource can also be found in Investopedia, which is exactly what the name sounds like: a comprehensive and understandable encyclopedia for investment. Some of these websites have apps that will allow investors to receive alerts on their phones when a significant financial event occurs. Of course, investors will get a taste for their own preferred websites as they become more comfortable in the finance world.

Opportunities at Home

Perhaps the most alluring aspect of binary options trading is what it allows investors to do with their lives. Starting out in investment can be difficult; during lunch breaks and after work an investor may be constantly checking in on his or her investments or even may be changing his or her work schedule in order to accommodate trading. If the trader works hard enough and shows a talent for trading, eventually this will pay off and hopefully the trader will be able to quit his or her day job in order to primarily trade. Ideally the investor's returns will continue to increase his or her capital, allowing for financial freedom that was not possible with the old day job. From there, it is up to the individual to use that financial autonomy however he or she sees fit.

This is what gets many people interested in binary options trading. Unfortunately it also sometimes serves as a catalyst for the draining of funds by an overly hopeful investor. However, if the investor is cautious with his or her capital and realistic regarding the chances of a high win rate using binary options trading, this should not be a problem. When applied sensibly, the dream of monetary freedom can be the motivation needed to continue trading even after periods of loss and propel the trader into binary options trading success.

Chapter 4: Tools and Strategies

For those who are intimidated by the idea of making a financial decision based only upon charts and the chattering of the financial world, have no fear. There are a number of tools and strategies available to help predict market moves. While these do take some studying in order to fully absorb, they are valuable materials, some of which are available online through brokerages for the benefit of investors. However, many of these strategies, once memorized, can be used without the need for any charts or online programs.

Tools

The tools that are most often used by binary options traders are ones meant for technical analysis. Of course, time frame charts have already been explained and so investors should be looking into hourly, daily, and weekly reports that will reflect the market price averages, highs, and lows. When reading these charts as the information occurs, however, investors rely upon a particular tool called technical indicators.

The Business Dictionary defines technical indicators as "A technical analysis tool for measuring and interpreting market behavior. Technical indicators can measure any number of factors, including the number of shares traded, the ratio of stocks rising to those declining, and the number of stocks making a new high or low."[5] Because technical indicators can be made up of such a varying range of factors, there are several different indicators, just as there are different stock option indices and exchanges. The main indicators are the moving average convergence/divergence line (MACD), Bollinger Bands®, accumulation/distribution line (A/D), pivot points, and the stochastic oscillator.

- **MACD**

    This average is set up by the trader and compares both short-term and long-term averages for the same stock in order to predict future trends. Additionally, this technical indicator will indicate the momentum of the stock, which can help traders to decide whether there is a chance of the trend reversing itself.[6]

- **Bollinger Bands®**

    This will literally look like a band on the graph with one line above the trend line and another line below. Created by John Bollinger in the 1980's, this indicator is used to predict when the market is about to enter a period of high volatility. They can also be used to determine how strong a trend is.[7]

- **A/D Line**

    This indicator is best used in the short-term and is used to predict whether money is being put into or being taken out of a particular security. The line will move upwards when money is coming in and downwards when it is going out. The reason it is best used in the short-term is because the line will move alongside the trend line and only marginally faster, allowing for very quick predictions. If this is paired with what the trader believes will soon be a high volatility market, then it may be a good time to make a trade.[8]

- **Pivot Points**

    Pivot points work in correlation with support and resistance levels. These levels are determined by a calculation taking the highs and lows of market prices into account. By observing the support and resistance levels, traders can speculate when a trend is about to break out of the level, hence pivoting. When the trend breaks out, new support and resistance levels are calculated and displayed automatically.[9]

- **Stochastic Oscillator**

    Here is another indicator that is used to predict momentum in a trend. The stochastic oscillator has been a primary indicator since it's invention in the 1950's and also uses support and resistance levels to calculate the potential market moves. Specifically, the stochastic oscillator takes into account the closing price of a particular security and then compares it to the highest and lowest points that security has experienced in the last 14 days. This indicator can also be used to observe when a security is overbought or oversold.[10]

Strategies

Implementing a strategy in binary options is more complicated than simply stating yes or no regarding the closing prices. In order to execute one successfully, investors need to be aware of the market climate and whether the security is acting bullish or bearish. Bullish refers to markets that are on the uptrend while bearish markets see a decrease in the value of the security. Here are a few strategies frequently used by investors. Readers should be aware that a combination of strategies is most likely to succeed since each security is different and may have a unique market climate.

- **Pinocchio**

    This is the most basic strategy there is and is the one that has been previously discussed. Essentially, if a security looks like it will increase, then traders should enter a call option. If it looks like it will drop, traders should enter a put option. Determining in which direction it will move can depend upon technical indicators, financial news, or other factors.[11]

- **Trend Line**

  In order to predict market movements, it can be helpful to use a trend line strategy, in which a trend line is drawn to mark the movements of a security. When the security looks like it will cross the trend line, it is usually reversing. Whether a trader enters a call or put option depends on whether the security is reversing upwards or downwards and how strong the move is likely to be.[12]

- **The Gap**

  It is not odd to sometimes see a gap in a chart, where the market price line has suddenly broken off and restarted at a new spot. These gaps often are not very large but they do often foreshadow a shift in the action of traders. If there is a gap in which a price suddenly jumps (whether that be because of some financial news or a break in trading) upwards, the gap is bound to close again and it may be wise for the investor to enter a put option.[13] If the gap shows a drop in price, then the opposite is true and the investor should enter a call option. The investor should determine how quickly this reversal in the price of the security will occur and thus, which time frame to trade in.

- **The Breakout**

The breakout strategy is dependent upon the trader's ability to predict when a trend will reverse. It is made easier with the help of indicators such as the bull and bear flags, pennants, triangles, rectangles, and wedges. In short, these are shapes that a market price line may take. If the trader spots one of these shapes, he or she takes note of it, adding the indicator onto the graph. When the price of the security is about to break out of this shape, that is the time for investors to enter a call or put option, depending upon the direction of the price movement.

Using a combination of these tools and strategies, new investors can begin to hone their skills predicting the price movements of securities. Of course, intense study is recommended before putting these techniques into practice. Once mastered, however, using these strategies in the right situation will earn the investor profits in a high win rate. Of course, determining the right situations to use each strategy will only come from study and experience.

Chapter 5: Getting Started

While it is of the extreme importance to be well prepared before entering the field of binary options trading, studying from a book will only take a new investor so far. At some point, theory becomes reality and the new investor must put his or her newfound education to use. That is where the question of platforms and brokers come in. Many hopeful new investors leap at the chance to trade with low risk to themselves, but this is inevitably where they end up failing. This chapter is designed to make readers aware of the pitfalls so many others have fallen to and help readers to avoid them. As it turns out, binary options trading can be a financially disastrous game before so much as entering a trade.

Platforms and Fraud

Unfortunately, this chapter must begin with a word of warning. While there is an abundance of convenient and apparently cheap trading platforms to be found online, the majority of these are scams. The problem has manifested to such magnitude that the U.S. Commodity Futures Trading Commission issued a warning to investors alerting them of binary options platforms that "allegedly include refusing to credit customer accounts, denying fund reimbursement, identity theft, and manipulation of software to generate losing trades."[14] This statement confirms any sneaking suspicions that may creep up when conducting online research that the majority of websites are far from reputable. Thus, it is best to only trade using platforms attached to established and trusted companies.

If there is ever any doubt regarding the authenticity and reliability of a trading platform, it is best for investors to abandon that particular avenue entirely. Some websites will purport that a binary options trading platform is reliable according to a government website, such as the U.S. Securities and Exchange Commission. However, once one has searched through the website, no mention can be found of the binary options platform in question. It is evident then that traders must always double check the authenticity of the platform they are interested in and often they must be prepared for disappointment.

It should be noted that these platform scams are not always obvious and those who are trying to break into the financial world are particularly susceptible to falling for these ploys. This may particularly apply to apprentice traders who have a substantial capital. New investors should not only be wary of scam websites but also of individuals seeking traders out in order to invite them to trade on their private platform. The investigation of such a scam was put to an end in 2012 when William Graulich was found guilty of inviting individuals to take part in his non-existent investment platform that touted astronomically high returns with no risk. This, of course, ended in the victims losing a substantial amount of money.[15]

Another such case resulted in a warning from the U.S. Securities and Exchange Commission (SEC) stating that investors should be wary of binary options trading platforms and the risks they entail. A Cyprus-based company that ran such a platform was recently charged with illegally selling options to American investors.[16] One type of scam that American investors have been falling for are platforms that are based in a foreign country that are not abiding by United States laws and regulations and are failing to report securities to the government. This should make investors especially wary of online platforms, particularly those that supposedly trade on the forex market. Clearly, double-checking the validity of online platforms is paramount to binary options survival. For example, that Cyprus-based company is named Blanc de Binary Ltd. It demonstrations one of the most trusted binary trading platforms by a company that supposedly reveals binary platform scams.

Here is a final word on the matter from Director of the SEC's Office of Investor Education and Advocacy, Lori Schock: "Investors should be aware of the potential for fraud in this area as well as of the reality that they can lose their entire investment... We strongly encourage investors to check the background of brokers and advisers and trading platforms before making a decision to invest. If investors can't obtain simple background information such as whether the financial professional is registered with the SEC or FINRA [Financial Industry Regulatory Authority], then they should be extremely wary."[17] In short, investors always need to do a kind of background check on potential partners and if something seems off, run in the other direction.

So how does an individual trade binary options if it is so impossible to get a reliable platform? Many of the times, the only solution to this problem is to go through a licensed brokerage. Doing so allows for not only assurance on the part of the investor that they are not taking part in an illegal scam, but also for a wealth of resources that may enhance a new trader's ability to sharpen his or her trading skills.

Brokers

When researching brokers, investors should be sure to keep their options open and thoroughly investigate each company. Investors should set up meetings with companies such as Charles Schwab, Scottrade, Fidelity Investments, and TD Ameritrade and speak with someone to inquire what packages may be available for binary options trading and what tools they give investors access to, like charts and indicators. Trading with companies such as these will give investors automatic peace of mind that they are not being taken advantage of and may offer additional tools to aid preparation before beginning to actually trade.

Of course, brokers will only allow an investor to utilize their resources if the investor creates an account and pays membership fees and commissions. These fees may vary but always involve a "commission per trade." For example, Fidelity offers online options trades for the price of $7.95 plus an additional $0.75 per contract. In contrast, Charles Schwab offers membership for $8.95 with an additional $0.75 per trade. While Fidelity may look like the better monetary deal, it's important to look into what benefits and resources are included. In general, the higher the commission rate is, the better the service, though of course there will always be companies looking to take advantage of unaware newcomers. Other fees may be written into the contract details, such as annual fees, maintenance fees, and fees for not maintaining a minimum balance, which can become a problem for those whose trading is not going well.

Additionally, most brokerages require a minimum deposit in order to open an account, much like a bank. This can be a wide range from a few hundred dollars to thousands of dollars. Hence, it is important for new investors to build up capital before entering the world of binary options trading. Of course, if that level of capital is simply not possible, there are some discount brokerages available.

Some traders may be debating whether they actually need a broker to trade. The fact of the matter is, unless a trader is physically on the floor of the stock market, they must have a broker to enter and exit deals on their behalf. Selecting a broker, however, should not be as simple as weighing the pros and cons of the brokerage. Novice traders should think of a broker like a lawyer: the broker needs to be trusted by both the trader and the institution, needs to have enough experience to impart financial wisdom, and should be trusted to keep the trader's monetary interests.

Though it may be intimidating to select a broker, traders should remember that signing with a brokerage does not mean that the trader is stuck with that broker permanently. If the trader is unhappy after testing out the brokerage, it is always acceptable to leave and sign with another one. Though traders should be careful to read the fine print when signing contracts to ensure that there is no fee for leaving and if there is, find out what time frame the fee is dependent on.

It is evident from this reading that the only trustworthy platform tends to be the one associated with a reliable brokerage. While commissions and fees do pose a challenge to new traders without a large capital sum, the payoff is far more rewarding than the brokerage's less lucrative counterparts. Those who wish to succeed in binary options trading should take into consideration every facet of a partnership with a broker so that they can optimize their chances for success in the trading field. Such determination and thoroughness can only make traders more formidable.

Chapter 6: Tips, Tricks, and Temperament

According to an article by CNN Money released in 2015, 48% of all Americans have money in stocks.[18] Now remove the vast majority of those people and what is left are those who make a living trading on the stock market. Those who can achieve this in any trading medium possess a quality that other traders do not: the right attitude. This chapter will take readers through the ideal qualities in a binary option trader as well as the practical tips that will help new investors get started on the right foot.

Temperament

So what exactly is the right attitude for a binary options trader? Well, there are a multitude of characteristics that might make up a particular trader; decisiveness and cunning are two that may come to mind when imagining the top binary options players. The attributes listed below are characteristics that every trader must have if they wish to make it in the world of investment.

- **Patience**

    Starting out in binary options will take more patience than those who know what they are doing and are beginning to amass a large amount of capital. Traders will need to have patience to get through low periods when experiencing a string of losses and the slow crawl upwards to a place where the trader's capital is substantial enough to begin diversifying the types of options he or she trades in.

- **Adaptability**

    The trader who is able to change the way they trade is the one who can stay on top of their game over the years. Future investors should recognize the value of using different strategies for different contracts, be aware of how the market and the technology used for it evolves, and be willing to throw out methods that don't work.

- **Humility**

    Along with the ability to adapt comes a heavy dose of humility. It is impossible to become an expert binary options trader if the investor is arrogant and believes that he or she cannot be beat. Even if the trader has gone twenty trades without losing, he or she needs to recognize that a loss is just around the corner. The looming loss will become much worse if the trader becomes too attached to specific strategies and ignores the chart indicators in favor of the winning strategy. Nobody can beat the market every time. Hence, humility is key.

- **Drive**

Readers who are interested in a career in binary options should take a moment to consider if they truly want this career. Yes, binary options has made people fortunes before, but it is a long road uphill to that kind of financial freedom and only those with the determination to put their nose to the grindstone day in and day out will get there. That kind of endurance is much, much harder to muster if the trader does not actually enjoy trading. So before an investor decides to take on the field, they need to be sure that they actually like the work.

- **Money Management Skills**

    Those who do not have the ability to manage multiple increments of money at the same time will not fare well at trading. However, those who do can improve their skill by using a log to mark all trades. Those entries should include day of the contract, the time, and strike price, price of the contract, closing price, strategy used, indicators used, and outcome. The log should also be used to balance the capital account, marking how much money is going towards commissions and fees, how much is being lost, and how much is being gained. This will keep the trader from running out of capital and taking unnecessary risks.

- **Confidence**

    As discussed in an earlier chapter, there is no way to generate an income trading binary options without suffering some loss. What separates amateur traders from masterful ones is not being afraid of loss. This does not mean that successful traders take unnecessary risks, but that they realize loss is a part of the industry and that the industry cannot exist without both losers and winners. Every trader experiences being in both positions, but that do not keep prosperous traders from participating.

- **A Cool Head**

    Trading involves almost constant highs and lows of emotion; at least, that may be the case initially. Succeeding at the majority of trades will naturally cause a trader to become excited and motivated to seek out further opportunities in the market, just as a succession of losses may cause a trader to reconsider his or her career. While the latter is sometimes the right course of action, traders usually just need to keep a calm temperament. Leaving emotions out of the equation allows traders to view the movement of the market objectively and enter the contracts with the best chance for a profit. Perhaps the worst outcome of letting emotions gain control is when a trader becomes so distraught over losses that they double up trying to make back lost money. In contrast to this, a trader who is doing exceptionally well may forget his or her humility and end up losing the capital he or she built up in a bad trade that could have easily been avoided.

Tips and Tricks

Below you will find a few helpful tips to help novice traders avoid binary options trading pitfalls.

1. Before beginning trading, investors should inquire from their brokerage if they can practice on a simulator. Not all brokerages may have this, but if they do it will allow the trader to go through the motions of entering and exiting a trade prior to actually trading. While the simulator will not recreate the emotional experience of trading, it will hopefully make traders more comfortable when they finally sit down to start trading.

2. Until a trader becomes proficient at binary options, he or she should keep things simple. Don't play options against each other on the forex or get caught up in strategies that involve too many moving pieces. Instead, traders should master the

basic skills and then build upon them. After all, in binary options the trader either wins $0 or $100, so it doesn't matter how fancy the strategy is; a simple strategy will earn a trader just as much money as a complicated one.

3. A good way for traders to reach their goals is to determine exactly what those goals are. This may sound redundant, but it is difficult to reach a goal when the individual isn't explicitly aware of what he or she wants. Readers should think of it this way: suppose that a trader named Bill determines that he wants to quit his day job within two years. Bill will need to calculate how much money is necessary to save up in order to begin generating a substantial income trading binary options. Then Bill will need to determine how much he needs to make each day and thus, how much money he needs to accrue per trade, accounting for inevitable losses,

commissions, and fees. If Bill sticks to the plan and proves to have a talent for binary options, then he ought to be able to reach his goal and be working as a full-time binary options trader within the desired two years timeline. Now consider this: if Bill had not set up a game plan to achieve these goals, how long could it have taken him to accomplish them?

4. Traders must always be able to trust their gut. This leads to a very important piece of advice: trust your broker, but don't get lazy. Yes the broker is there to make calls and puts on behalf of the investor, and to offer advice (and hopefully if the trader trusts his or her broker, the broker is very good at their job), but the win/loss ratio is ultimately up to the investor and if the investor does not stay up to date with financial news and current trends, he or she will undoubtedly lose money.

5. Gaining steam in binary options can be an agonizingly slow process. Despite the frustrations that accompany this, traders must learn to take their time. Traders who want to succeed should not try to speed things up or sign a contract with the first brokerage they get on the phone with. The advice to keep a cool head extends to this brokerage interview stage and the selection of securities. The vital thing you should remember is that each preparatory stage of binary options trading will have a significant role in the success or failure of the trader's endeavor. Thus, traders must take their time and make selections with care. After all, these initial choices are what the career is built upon.

Will these tips make a novice into an efficacious trader? No, they will not. What these tips and suggestions will do is give an advantage to the prospective trader who is truly willing to learn, adapt, and be committed to a career in binary options trading. Those prepared to take on the challenges of trading should follow these suggestions so that when the time comes to actually put money on the table, investors can enter the trade with a cool head and informed mind which, in the end, will lead them to monetary success.

Conclusion

Thank you again for downloading this book!

I hope this book was able to help you gain a better understanding of binary options and how to succeed trading them. Over recent years, binary options trading has earned its place among other investment opportunities that have made participants millions of dollars. While many have flocked to this reemerging field in hopes of quickly accumulating a fortune, most have been disappointed. This is not because trading binary options is an impossible field to succeed in. Rather, so many have failed because they were not properly educated before entering the trade, did not have a natural talent for investment, and fell prey to scams promising great rewards with little to no risk.

The next step is to ensure that this definition does not apply to you. With the proper tools, it is possible to make a lucrative career out of binary options. This book has given readers the necessary tools to begin, ranging from the importance of an ongoing education to the danger of online platforms. Those who make a study of the strategies, indicators, and market movements as well as keep accurate track of their funds will find themselves at a huge advantage, making them able to not only compete but also understand their mistakes. Correcting those mistakes and continuing to move forward with dedication and perseverance make up some of the core traits of a prosperous trader. Recognizing those trait requirements as a newcomer makes individual traders all the more likely to succeed.

Binary options trading can be a fantastic avenue to financial freedom, giving traders the ability to quit their day jobs, take vacations, and pay off mortgages early. While it may not be the easiest avenue, those that possess natural investment talent and who are prepared to work for success can make it happen. This book has given readers insight on how to begin; now all that is left to do is get started and begin a career as a professional binary options trader today.

Finally, if you enjoyed this book, please take the time to share your thoughts and post a review on Amazon. It'd be greatly appreciated!

Thank you and good luck!

[1] Mitchell, Corey. "A Guide To Trading Binary Options In The U.S." *Investopedia.* Investopedia, 17 Mar. 2016. Web. 2 July 2016.

[2] Harrison, Charlie. "10 Step Guide to Binary Options Trading." *Binary Options: Guide to Options Trading.* Top10Binary, n.d. Web. 2 July 2016.

[3] Harrison, Charlie. "Types of Binary Options." *Binary Options: Guide to Options Trading.* Top10Binary, n.d. Web. 2 July 2016.

[4] Dumon, Marvin. "An Overview of Commodities Trading." *Investopedia.* Investopedia, n.d. Web. 2 July 2016.

[5] "Technical Indicator." *BusinessDictionary.com.* BusinessDictionary.com, n.d. Web. 3 July 2016.

[6] Fowlkes, Michael. "5 Technical Indicators Every Trader Should Know." *Money Show: Invest Smarter. Trade Wiser.* Money Show, 27 Feb. 2015. Web. 3 July 2016.

[7] "Bollinger Bands® Introduction." *Bollinger Bands®,* Bollinger Bands®, n.d. Web. 3 July 2016.

[8] Fowlkes, Michael. "5 Technical Indicators Every Trader Should Know." *Money Show: Invest Smarter. Trade Wiser.* Money Show, 27 Feb. 2015. Web. 3 July 2016.

[9] "Pivot Point Trading." *Binary Options University.* Binary Options U, n.d. Web. 3 July 2016.

[10] "Stochastic Indicator." *Investopedia.* Investopedia, n.d. Web. 3 July 2016.

[11] Miller, John. "Strategies." *7 Binary Options.* 7 Binary Options, n.d. Web. 3 July 2016.

[12] Miller, John. "Strategies." *7 Binary Options.* 7 Binary Options, n.d. Web. 3 July 2016.

[13] "Gap Strategy." *Binary Options Strategy.* Binary Options Strategy, n.d. Web. 3 July 2016.

[14] "CFTC Fraud Advisories." *U.S. Commodity Futures Trading Commission: Ensuring the Integrity of the Futures and Swaps Markets.* U.S. Commodity Futures Trading Commission, n.d. Web. 3 July 2016.

[15] Singer, Bill. "Another Trading Platform Scam Ends in Prison." *Forbes.* Forbes, 18 May 2012. Web. 3 July 2016.

[16] U.S. Securities and Exchange Commission. Newsroom. *SEC Warns Investors About Binary Options and Charges Cyprus-Based Company with Selling Them Illegally in U.S. SEC.gov.* United States Government, 6 June 2013. Web. 3 July 2016.

[17] U.S. Securities and Exchange Commission. Newsroom. *SEC Warns Investors About Binary Options and Charges Cyprus-Based Company with Selling Them Illegally in U.S. SEC.gov.* United States Government, 6 June 2013. Web. 3 July 2016.

[18] Long, Heather. "Over half of American have $0 in stocks." *CNN Money.* Time Warner, 10 Apr. 2015. Web. 3 July 2016.

www.ingramcontent.com/pod-product-compliance
Lightning Source LLC
Chambersburg PA
CBHW060408190526
45169CB00002B/804